E L E C T R I C
D E S E R T S

poems by

Amber McCrary

Jackalope Chaps
Coconino, Mojave, & Sonora

Electric Deserts

Edited by Heather Lang-Cassera.

Cover art and design by David Pischke.
Cover photography by Brandi Pischke.

Set in Arechetype 11 pt font.
Design by David Pischke.

ISBN 978-1-948800-31-0

Published by Jackalope Chaps, an imprint of Tolsun Publishing, Inc. Flagstaff, Arizona & Las Vegas, Nevada.
www.tolsunbooks.com

CONTENTS

ELECTRIC DESERTS!

A MIXTAPE FOR A 30-SOMETHING-YEAR-OLD PUNK GIRL

Give me the 30-year-old punk
with experience
Give me the 30-year-old punk of color
unafraid of the skinny white boy
testing my 1970s record collection
The Slits were more punk
than the Sex Pistols
founded by a now-ridiculous Johnny Rotten
and racist-ass, Sid Vicious

Give me the Diné girl giggling
in the alley all in black
reclaiming her sexuality
at every turn

Give me the 30-year-old
Navajo punk still listening
to her X's records, skipping
from all the scratches
letting the blood pulse in this body of anger

Give me the shy Navajo goth girl
unaware of her worth
her driving that used to scare the shit out of me
her kindness louder than Al Jorgenson's smashing screams

Give me the loud Navajo girl
quick to punch, slow to flower
our red blood molds us in these alleys

white and red
such a strange concoction of violence
sparkling with unending nerves

Leather on leather
black jeans crusted with holes
Dead Kennedy Patches, slaps of dead hair dedicated to Danzig
sponged with iridescent valours

Kick this 40 oz into gear
and throw me into the swirl of
stinky white and brown bodies
Let me be confused by my anger
Let me be confused by the racism
Let me be confused by the sexism
Let me be confused by dreams of escaping all that I know

Give me this body I have now
that understands it was a dream to be confused in my own curiosity
with a kickass mixtape
letting my brain shrink in all the alcohol, drugs, & romance of dead

Give me this 30-year-old body living
Give me this 30-year-old punk lady
Still dreaming of the world beyond that alley in that small town
Give me all that is forgotten

Give me what I hoped to forget
and let's celebrate

ELECTRIC DESERTS

A quiet storm
               A gentle giant
                              Smooth sands swirl

Filling my sky with silt
tensions crackle with dry lightning

Two deserts collide
Sonoran and Colorado Plateau

Electric faults
               Electric tensions
                              Electric weathering

The neighbors can hear
but we don't care

The high and low plains of our asses
create a journey
that cannot be paved or measured in miles

There is no sign to these electric deserts
tourists cannot pay to see these cosmic lands
sorry to say to *your* masses

But our red asses
are for our eyes only, tonight

Cactus, yucca, aloe, juniper, sage and creosote collide
mixing thousands of years of medicine
millennial years with no pay, no pain, no license

The origin of your desert flourishes
in the canyons of my pelvis
erodes the bitterness of my breakage

We are not our wilderness
but our plentitude

COMPANION

You're my favorite thing
a line from the Replacements
plays from the stereo
first edition pressing, yum
my ears say, watch the vinyl

> My onyx vinyl twirls
> I fluff the wires behind
> the speaker making
> sound cleaner for dirty guitars
> to belch out into the air

Angry white boy music
this angry brown girl in love
mountain Diné punk
brews in nostalgia
the sweetest tea dances tan

> In the winds blue air
> the deepest green dances home
> tickles and twirls
> the sinuses in my nose
> pollen makes me feel sleepy
> find me in the green dreaming

Find me lavender
Find me reading purple
Finding me bathing pink
Find me synthesizing blue
Find me sipping peacock tongues

BLUE CORN CUPCAKE EATER
(NATIVE GIRLS NEED LOVE, TOO!)

To see him,
I walk through countless doors
smelly, shiny hallways
and quiet hallow pods
of a small reservation high school

High desert love hides in his smile, Diné Bikeyah
Low desert fascination climbs onto my shoulder, O'odham Bikeyah
Soundful awes sparkle in silky, spicy sand
and a tribe's fondness for George Strait and dually trucks
Delightful finds coo in the ocotillos, palo verdes and saguaros
and a people's love for chicken scratch and dancing in circles for hours

My hunger pangs
want to bestow you
but all week I have only
seen the worry and strain
in your eyes
gasping for ease
like a tumbleweed between your ears
as strands of hair
Indigenous as mesquite
fall onto your caramel forehead

I avert, sit in your classroom, cross my legs
& let you be

All week I think about
a moment where your eyes lower
turn to hazel

then you remember
who I am

I seen it before
& it is what brings me back every time

I bring you blue corn cupcakes
for your heartaches
You take one cupcake
and bite into the periwinkle bread
I try not to stare
too loudly
as I converse
about nothing

You stop
and listen
with each bite
and respond with
gumption and gut

Then I remember who you are
I bake my blue corn desert
for your Sonoran palms
to place and digest
in your saguaro belly

You don't have to guess
what this blue corn girl is suggesting

DESERT DERRIÈRE

Its fluffy, billowiness like baby cheeks
is the derrière of my homesickness
the pit of stiffness

Its glazed, homemade dinner roll derrière
dawns on the horizon of my slapping hand

Rather a massaging-like hand
not a finger or nail
to display light strawberry streaks across skin

For my desert derrière
must always have gusts
have an uncreased sand dune

Each grain falls into place
creates a perfect butt of a hill

I do not want to shovel or mark it with pity
but with rain from my tongue to skin

Do not mistake my diligence for
unfulfilled lust
but filled wildness

Filled savagery like a twinkie
sticky, sweet and unapologetic

But give me some credit
this little Indigenous gal
likes to wravoc a little hell

No dairy air ever comes out of this divine derrière
rather noises in the bathroom
that it thinks I do not hear

So I laugh in the bedroom
because it's my happiest moments not known
even to the desert derrière of my desire

I have to say from time to time it sets me on fire

LILAC PORTALS

Worlds within me jump into the sky
I hear the pulsating glitter spinning in me
origins of energy tinker in my spine

Rain vibrates in my hand
digging for the lines
Canal stories flow through
the grooves of my pink palms

                 My hands touch the ground

Portals of seasonal love
distinguish me in earth
flood my husks with worth

Wash me down the river
& collect me when you are home

                 Move your batch of visions
                 into my mounting palms

Release the birds from their portal
Do not crush the seeds
Let the birds find them
when they wake from the sky

ROUND DANCE RAIN

The muse of my desert
the dessert of my muse
I want to eat all the sands of your desert sweetness

Give me every grain in the whole Sonoran
I will crunch and swallow every bit
take the sweetness of the desert
place split saguaro fruit into my palms
and I will place it on the ground face up
Its sweetness returns to the sky
then back to my lips
and I will swing and stomp in a million circles for you

Our round dance brings the sweetest rain
It enters a circle
much like the sun
but within my throat I feel it
swirl into a million soft cacti
piercing each part of this sadness
and yearning
700 miles away

Take the spikes and put them in a bag
so they will retrieve the morose of my thoughts
and hang them on a wall for me to call art
For me to make a zine
For me to make a pie
For me to make a lie
A cactus frame

of your face in the middle
because in the forest of my dreams
I lay in it
and I'm living in it

A LETTER TO THE LAND

Apologizing to the land is apologizing to my body
I wonder if Mother Earth wished it were white as a little girl?
I want to tell the little girl in me, it will soon switch
      its conditioned thoughts
You will find comfort in your body as you are with the land

Apologizing to my body is apologizing to the land
I'm sorry when I was a young girl when our family would go
      to visit grandma
I saw Diné Bikeyah as desolate, nothing, somewhere we
      are taught to escape
Little would I know, I would travel the world and always think
      of grandma
in the tangerine canyons
living how she always wanted to

How do I apologize to the land and my body in Navajo
when there is such word in my mother tongue?
How do I show or plea forgiveness
in a place I saw as inferior?
I take my hands and smooth the folds and roundness
that make up my skin given to me from the holy people
They paint the sky and land
and give us our four mountains to live near, always
They paint our bodies to never be ashamed to remember
We come from the cosmic energies of Father Sky and Mother Earth
How do I say I'm a fool looking for beauty in a land stolen
A body stolen
How do I take my hands and open them
clasp them and sprinkle celebration

HE

BODY—BRAIN—FOG

He wakes up
& rips the IVs out of his skin
His body bogged

His anxiety controls the bottle
& the bottle wants to be friends with his head
They become best buds
They become blood

The alcohol in his blood
wakes in sleezy hotels,
cold trailers,
hospital beds,
ambulance rides,
cop cars,
& jail cells.

The blood of his K'e sees him walk
downtown to find K'e with other Diné men,
They hand him a bottle of Old English
he drinks in a circle, camaraderie, "generosity."

The circle breaks when
the first punch is thrown
Pain peels out from their skin
into fists balled onto faces
into the traumatic air.

Where else to go?
Jail. Downtown. Jail. Downtown.
sleep.drink.sleep.drink.

love.simple.love.simple.
family.home.family.home.

Soaked nerves dry
his libations lied

Where is your home, brother?

Haadî Nighan Shinaaí?

HOME VISIT

Mom
> "He wasn't as drunk this time"
> "He doesn't get belligerent like he used to"
> "He just goes to sleep now"

Grandma
> "Wow! Look at you, you've gained weight"
> "I'm tired of my elders dying"
> "I can't drive home tonight"
> "This poem is about me?" ::laughs::

Dad
> "I had an older half brother, he disappeared when I was 17,
> Some say he is still alive, living in skid row.
> No one knows what happened to him. That was 40 years ago"
> "He had an arranged marriage and only lasted two days"

Brother
> "Sorry, I'm sorry"

LIQUID LOVE

This wheel of circuitous
is what keeps me spinning

Liquid leaves titillate
dormant musings
in this cave I call a skull

Laughter arches above me
one spring step heaves
below ground
alone, takes me by the hand
moss and mess
I'm neither here nor there

SETTLER MOVES TO INNOCENCE

Shake loose these excuses
blinded as strong undercurrents
of bored capitalism
& guilt without repair

Blameless settler
with orange trees
claims they were always
his to drink from
and always his to do with

Give me the fruit
and you can have the peels
for your children

I LIKE MY TEA LIKE I LIKE MY LAND

I love the taste of yerba mate
It tastes almost like Rez dirt after a rainstorm
When I was a little girl
I used to love the smell of wet Dinè Bikeyah dirt
This was usually in Shonto when it would rain
Sometimes I even ate the dirt which I don't regret
It's still one of the best things I've ever tasted
It must be why the land always calls me home
It knows the land is in my belly

It knows where my placenta
is buried
It knows
when my heart aches
It knows when I sip yerba mate
on this cold rainy day in the bay
and I think of its dirt
The color of yerba mate tea
The color of my grandma's laugh
The color of my brother's cheeks

A liquid amber
like a sheet over our skeletal dust
flowing in the distance
Somewhere in northern Arizona
that is where my dust settles

TC COINCIDENCE? I THINK NOT!

Twenty years and some change later
we meet and learn we both lived in the same
Rez trailer park
You know the one behind McDonalds
by the trading post
on Moenave St.

We laugh about it
because when you're poor
sitting in sadness is too easy
too dilapidating, we aren't easy people
Humor gives us another day to live for
Jokes only trailer park Rez kids understand

Your Tuba City slang
surprises me
snd I cackle
in bed, museums, bookstores, cafes, the car
in metropolises, suburbs, and little Rez towns
Twenty plus years later, we meet
Twenty plus years later, we are sweet
with one another

On the couch
you try to speak Navajo
with wide eyes
You grab my hips and say in your low voice
Shi heart, Shi Girl
I scream *Stop!*

I laugh so hard my cheeks would explode
if it weren't for my round hazelnut skin keeping them intact

You continue to repeat romantic Rez words and look into my eyes
My stomach is full of luxury, my brown belly wants to fart
        with laughter
But I yell *Stop!*
because I would be too embarrassed if my body reacted as such
The Rez kid in me has learned her limits

I move and sit on the floor of my living room
and browse through an early '90s edition of *Native People's Magazine*
A Michael Chiago painting serenades the glossy page
I hold it up and show the painting to you, it is of an O'odham village

Men and women are holding hands
They are in a circle side stepping with each beat
The Sonoran Desert in the background, purple mountains
        blend into the mango horizon
You say, *it looks nice,* smile and continue reading
        for your grad-school class
I look closer at the picture of the men in the painting
        Mr. Chiago is spot on
I say, *you could be one of the men in this, they look like you.*
You smirk because you think I'm making fun of you, but I am not
Your low, soft, sleepy O'odham eyes with broom-like eyelashes
        straight and thick
always manage to sweep me away
Your olive black shoulder-length hair and horizontal mouth
look like the T.O. grandpas round dancing in the painting,

I like to think of an old you, cheii you
your hands the color of theirs, hickory with darker hints at the
      knuckles and elbows

I close the magazine
and lay on the couch next to you
I want to interrupt you so bad
and play like rowdy Rez kids in the boonies
but we are now Indigenous grownups, living in the city,
      heirlooms of our nation, Dinè and O'odham
Reading and living toward a better future from what
      our mothers and fathers had
Alas, I get up and take a shower
so I do not disturb you

DINÉ GIRL SHINE

Harvest the blue corn
Tell the tan girls to beware
Protection pollen
Shuck the husks as coats
Let them see the world brightly

MONSOON MUSINGS

Fill me with your water
I see your gray clouds from afar
We aren't scared
yet celebratory
Your gray clouds, moving fast but not violent

Desert winds increase
as our hearts beat with excitement
This undulation of drops
comes fast as they leave

We wait all year for you
celebrate around your arrival
Olla's hollow for your yearly presence

We all muse into your monsoon
dance for hours
sing with throats uncollapsing
The sand dances for you in this stiff air

Fill us with your language
Fill us with your breath
Tell us you will come back

Then we will celebrate until the next time
Remember you as our muse
Remember you as our life
                                    our love

Amber McCrary is Diné poet, zinester and feminist. She is Red House born for Mexican people. Originally from Shonto, Arizona and raised in Flagstaff, Arizona. In the small town of Flagstaff is where she discovered her love for Punk Rock and the Do-It-Yourself Culture. She earned her BA from Arizona State University in Political Science with a minor in American Indian Studies. She is currently pursuing her MFA in poetry at Mills College. She is also the creator of *DANG! Zine (Daydreaming, Awkward, Native, Girl) Vol. 1* and *Vol.2*, *Angsty Asdzáá: Tales of an angry Indigenous womxn zine* and *The Asdzáá Beat*. She currently lives in Oakland, California.

CPSIA information can be obtained
at www.ICGtesting.com
Printed in the USA
BVHW030547050820
585523BV00002B/160

9 781948 800310